Improve r~~ skills and word comprehension and increase self esteem all while having fun!

Have fun, be silly, and practice word writing and reading comprehension, all at the same time!

More than 200 funny and hilarious jokes that will have kids laugh out loud

next pages contain - The most hilarious :

* JOKES
* Riddles
* Tongue Twisters
* Knock knock Jokes

For 5 years old Kids!

Funny Jokes is what all Kids love , before sleeping or during the day , even parents will share funny moments with their children

Lot Of Jokes!

What do you call a dinosaur that is sleeping?

A DINO-SNORE!

What is fast, loud and crunchy?

A ROCKET CHIP!

Why did the teddy bear say no to dessert?

BECAUSE SHE WAS STUFFED.

What has ears but cannot hear?

A CORNFIELD

What did the left eye say to the right eye?

BETWEEN US, SOMETHING SMELLS!

What do you get when you cross a vampire and a snowman?

FROST BITE!

What did one plate say to the other plate?

DINNER IS ON ME!

Why did the student eat his homework?

BECAUSE THE TEACHER TOLD HIM IT WAS A PIECE OF CAKE!

When you look for something, why is it always in the last place you look?

BECAUSE WHEN YOU FIND IT, YOU STOP LOOKING

What is brown, hairy and wears sunglasses?

A COCONUT ON VACATION

Two pickles fell out of a jar onto the floor. What did one say to the other?

DILL WITH IT.

What did the Dalmatian say after lunch?

THAT HIT THE SPOT!

Why did the kid cross the playground?

TO GET TO THE OTHER SLIDE.

How does a vampire start a letter?

TOMB IT MAY CONCERN...

What do you call a droid that takes the long way around?

R2 DETOUR.

How do you stop an astronaut's baby from crying?

YOU ROCKET!

Why was 6 afraid of 7?

BECAUSE 7, 8, 9

What is a witch's favorite subject in school?

SPELLING!

When does a joke become a "dad" joke?

WHEN THE PUNCHLINE IS A PARENT.

How do you make a lemon drop?

JUST LET IT FALL

What did the limestone say to the geologist?

DON'T TAKE ME FOR GRANITE!

What do you call a duck that gets all A's?

A WISE QUACKER

Why does a seagull fly over the sea?

BECAUSE IF IT FLEW OVER THE BAY, IT WOULD BE A BAYGULL.

What kind of water cannot freeze?

HOT WATER

What kind of tree fits in your hand?

A PALM TREE!

Why did the cookie go to the hospital?

BECAUSE HE FELT CRUMMY.

Why was the baby strawberry crying?

BECAUSE HER MOM AND DAD WERE IN A JAM

What did the little corn say to the mama corn?

WHERE IS POP CORN?

What is worse than raining cats and dogs?

HAILING TAXIS!

How much does it cost a pirate to get his ears pierced?

ABOUT A BUCK AN EAR

Where would you find an elephant?
THE SAME PLACE YOU LOST HER!

How do you talk to a giant?
USE BIG WORDS!

What animal is always at a baseball game?
A BAT

What falls in winter but never gets hurt?

SNOW!

What do you call a ghost's true love?

HIS GHOUL-FRIEND..

What building in New York has the most stories?

THE PUBLIC LIBRARY!

What did one volcano say to the other?

I LAVA YOU!

How do we know that the ocean is friendly?

IT WAVES!

What is a tornado's favorite game to play?

TWISTER!

How does the moon cut his hair?
ECLIPSE IT

How do you get a squirrel to like you?
ACT LIKE A NUT!

What do you call two birds in love?
TWEETHEARTS!

How does a scientist freshen her breath?

WITH EXPERI-MINTS!

How are false teeth like stars?

THEY COME OUT AT NIGHT!

How can you tell a vampire has a cold?

SHE STARTS COFFIN.

What's worse than finding a worm in your apple?

FINDING HALF A WORM.

What is a computer's favorite snack?

COMPUTER CHIPS!!

Why don't elephants chew gum?

THEY DO, JUST NOT IN PUBLIC.

What was the first animal in space?

THE COW THAT JUMPED OVER THE MOON

What did the banana say to the dog?

NOTHING. BANANAS CAN'T TALK.

What time is it when the clock strikes 13?

TIME TO GET A NEW CLOCK.

How does a cucumber become a pickle?

IT GOES THROUGH A JARRING EXPERIENCE.

What do you call a boomerang that won't come back?

A STICK.

What do you think of that new diner on the moon?

FOOD WAS GOOD, BUT THERE REALLY WASN'T MUCH ATMOSPHERE.

Why did the dinosaur cross the road?

BECAUSE THE CHICKEN WASN'T BORN YET.

Why can't Elsa have a balloon?

BECAUSE SHE WILL LET IT GO.

How do you make an octopus laugh?

WITH TEN-TICKLES!

How do you make a tissue dance?
YOU PUT A LITTLE BOOGIE IN IT.

What's green and can fly?
SUPER PICKLE!

What did the nose say to the finger?
QUIT PICKING ON ME!

What musical instrument is found in the bathroom?

A TUBA TOOTHPASTE.

Why did the kid bring a ladder to school?

BECAUSE SHE WANTED TO GO TO HIGH SCHOOL.

What is a vampire's favorite fruit?

A BLOOD ORANGE.

What do elves learn in school?
THE ELF-ABET.

What do you call a dog magician?
A LABRACADABRADOR.

Where do pencils go on vacation?
PENCIL-VANIA.

Why couldn't the pony sing a lullaby?

SHE WAS A LITTLE HOARSE.

Why didn't the skeleton go to the dance?

HE HAD NO BODY TO DANCE WITH.

What gets wetter the more it dries?

A TOWEL.

What do you call two bananas?
SLIPPERS.

Why did the banana go to the doctor?
BECAUSE IT WASN'T PEELING WELL.

What do you call a fake noodle?
AN IMPASTA.

What stays in the corner yet can travel all over the world?

A STAMP.

How do you fix a cracked pumpkin?

WITH A PUMPKIN PATCH.

What kind of award did the dentist receive?

A LITTLE PLAQUE.

What do you call a funny mountain?
HILL-ARIOUS.

Why are ghosts bad liars?
BECAUSE YOU CAN SEE RIGHT THROUGH THEM.

Why do bees have sticky hair?
BECAUSE THEY USE A HONEYCOMB.

What did the big flower say to the little flower?

HI, BUD!

What part of your body can cause the end of the world?

YOUR APOCO-LIPS

What did the astronaut say when he crashed into the moon?

"I APOLLO-GIZE."

Why didn't the orange win the race?

IT RAN OUT OF JUICE.

What dinosaur had the best vocabulary?

THE THESAURUS.

Why aren't dogs good dancers?

THEY HAVE TWO LEFT FEET.

What did the wolf say when it stubbed its toe?

OWWWWW-CH!

Why did Johnny throw the clock out of the window?

BECAUSE HE WANTED TO SEE TIME FLY.

Why did the man put his money in the freezer?

HE WANTED COLD HARD CASH!

Why couldn't the astronaut book a hotel on the moon?

BECAUSE IT WAS FULL.

How do pickles enjoy a day out?

THEY RELISH IT.

What do you call an old snowman?

WATER.

What's a pirate's favorite letter?

ARRRRRRRRR

What do you get when you cross an elephant with a fish?

SWIMMING TRUNKS.

How do you throw a party in space?

YOU PLANET.

What did zero say to eight?

NICE BELT!

What do you call a sleeping bull?

A BULLDOZER!

Why did the tomato blush?

IT SAW THE SALAD DRESSING.

What do you call a fish without an eye?

A FSH.

What's the difference between roast beef and pea soup?

ANYONE CAN ROAST BEEF.

Why did the tomato blush?

IT SAW THE SALAD DRESSING.

What do you get when you cross a centipede with a parrot?

A WALKIE TALKIE.

Why are robots never afraid?

THEY HAVE NERVES OF STEEL.

Why did the cabbage win the race?

BECAUSE IT WAS A-HEAD.

What do you get if you cross a pie and a snake?

A PIE-THON.

What do you do if you get peanut butter on your doorknob?

USE A DOOR JAM.

Why didn't the robot finish his breakfast?

BECAUSE THE ORANGE JUICE TOLD HIM TO CONCENTRATE.

Why can't you play hockey with pigs?

THEY ALWAYS HOG THE PUCK.

Why do porcupines always win the game?

THEY HAVE THE MOST POINTS.

Where do elephants pack their clothes?

IN THEIR TRUNKS!

What does bread do on vacation?
LOAF AROUND.

Why was the broom running late?
IT OVER-SWEPT.

What part of the fish weighs the most?
THE SCALES.

What do ghosts like to eat in the summer?

I SCREAM.

Why did the teacher wear sunglasses to school?

BECAUSE HER STUDENTS WERE SO BRIGHT.

What do you call a deer with pink eye?

A COLORFUL EYE-DEER

Where do sheep go on vacation?

THE BAAA-HAMAS.

What does every birthday end with?

THE LETTER Y.

What did the paper say to the pencil?

WRITE ON!

Why do birds fly?
IT'S FASTER THAN WALKING.

Why did the pillow cross the road?
IT WAS PICKING UP THE CHICKEN'S FEATHERS.

Can February March?
NO, BUT APRIL MAY.

What time do ducks wake up?

AT THE QUACK OF DAWN.

Why did the giraffes get bad grades?

SHE HAD HER HEAD IN THE CLOUDS.

What did the flower say after it told a joke?

I WAS JUST POLLEN YOUR LEG.

What did the traffic light say to the truck?

DON'T LOOK, I'M CHANGING.

What does a cloud wear?

THUNDERWEAR!

Why didn't the koala bear get the job?

THEY SAID SHE WAS OVER-KOALA-FIED.

Who was that owl who did all the tricks?

WHO-DINI.

What kind of vegetable is angry?

A STEAMED CARROT!

How does the moon stay up in the sky?

MOONBEAMS!

Why isn't there a clock in the library?

BECAUSE IT TOCKS TOO MUCH.

Why do you never see elephants hiding in trees?

BECAUSE THEY'RE SO GOOD AT IT!

What day of the week are most twins born on?

TWOS-DAY!

What do you call bears with no ears?

B.

Where do rocks like to sleep?

BEDROCKS!

How do you pay for parking in space?

A PARKING METEOR.

What do you call two giraffes colliding?

A GIRAFFE-IC JAM.

What did the reporter say to the ice cream?

"WHAT'S THE SCOOP?"

How do you get fired from a coin-mint?

YOU STOP MAKING CENTS.

What room is impossible to enter?
A MUSHROOM.

What do you call cheese that's not yours?
NACH-O CHEESE."

What did the hat say to the scarf?
YOU HANG AROUND, AND I'LL GO AHEAD.

KNOCK KNOCK JOKES

Knock, knock.
Who's there?
Cow-go.
Cow-go who?
No, cow go MOO!

Knock, knock.
Who's there?
Goat.
Goat who?
Goat to the door and find out.

Knock, knock.
Who's there?
Honey bee.
Honey bee who?
Honey bee a dear and get me some water.

Knock, knock.
Who's there?
Interrupting cow.
Interrupting cow (you yell MOOOOOO! Before they can finish)

Knock, knock.
Who's there?
Interrupting sloth.
Interrupting sloth who?
(wait for 10-20 seconds)Sloooooooooth

Knock, knock.
Who's there?Monkey.
Monkey who?
Monkey see. Monkey do.

Knock, knock.
Who's there?
Owls say.
Owls say who?
Yes, they do.

Knock, knock.
Who's there?
Rough.
Rough who?
Rough, rough, rough! It's your dog!.

Knock, knock.
Who's there?
Some bunny.
Some bunny who?
Some bunny has been
eating all my carrots!

Knock, knock.
Who's there?
Who.
Who who?
Is there an owl in here?

Knock, knock.
Who's there? Havana.
Havana who?
Havana a wonderful time wish you were here!

Knock, knock.
Who's there? Juneau.
Juneau who?
Juneau the capital of Alaska?

Knock, knock.
Who's there?
Kenya.
Kenya who?
Kenya feel the love tonight? (sing along!)

Knock, knock.
Who's there?
Oslo.
Oslo who?
Oslo down, what's the hurry!?

Knock, knock.
Who's there?
Venice.
Venice who?
Venice your mom coming home?

Knock, knock.
Who's there?
Adore.
Adore who?
Adore is between us. Open up!

Knock, knock.
Who's there?
Alien.
Alien who?
Just how many aliens do you know?

Knock, knock.
Who's there?
Amish.
Amish who?
Awe, I miss you too.

Knock, knock.
Who's there?
Atch.
Atch who?
Bless you!

Knock, knock.
Who's there?
Avenue.
Avenue who?
Avenue knocked on this door before?

Knock, knock.
Who's there?
Bed.
Bed who?
Bed you can't guess who I am!

Knock, knock.
Who's there?
Boo.
Boo? who?
I didn't mean to make you cry!

Knock, knock.
Who's there?
Broken pencil.
Broken pencil who?
Never mind, it's pointless!

Knock, knock.
Who's there?
Burglar.
Burglar who?
Burglars don't knock!

Knock, knock.
Who's there?
Canoe.
Canoe who?
Canoe come out and play today?

Knock, knock.
Who's there?
Cash.
Cash who?
No thanks, but I'll take a peanut.

Knock, knock.
Who's there?
Cargo.
Cargo who?
Cargo beep, beep, vroom, vroom!

Knock, knock.
Who's there?
Comb.
Comb who?
Comb on down, and I'll tell you!

Knock, knock.
Who's there?
Dishes.
Dishes who?
Dishes a nice place you got here.

Knock, knock.
Who's there?
Doctor.
Doctor who?
You've seen that TV show?

Knock, knock.
Who's there?
Dozen.
Dozen who?
Dozen anyone want to let me in?

Knock, knock.
Who's there?
From.
From who?
Grammatically speaking, you should say "from whom."

Knock, knock.
Who's there?
Leaf.
Leaf who?
Leaf me alone!

Knock, knock.
Who's there?
Little old lady.
Little old lady who?
I didn't know you could yodel.

Knock, knock.
Who's there?
Mustache.
Mustache who?
I mustache you a question,
but I'll shave it for later.

Knock, knock.
Who's there?
Needle.
Needle who?
Needle little help gettin' in
the door.

Knock, knock.
Who's there?
Nun.
Nun who?
Nun of your business!

Knock, knock.
Who's there?
Police.
Police who?
Police (please) may I come in?

Knock, knock.
Who's there?
Police.
Police who?
Police hurry—I'm freezing
out here!

Knock, knock.
Who's there?
Radio.
Radio who?
Radio not, here I come!

Knock, knock.
Who's there?
Scold.
Scold who?
Scold outside—let me in!

Knock, knock.
Who's there?
Spell.
Spell who?
W-H-O!

Knock, knock.
Who's there?
Tank.
Tank who?
You're welcome!

Knock, knock.
Who's there?
Wa.
Wa who?
What are YOU so excited about?

Knock, knock.
Who's there?
Water.
Water who?
Water you doing in my house?

Knock, knock.
Who's there?
Witches.
Witches who?
Witches the way to the store?

Knock, knock.
Who's there?
Wooden shoe.
Wooden shoe who?
Wooden shoe like to hear another joke?

Knock, knock.
Who's there?
Zoom.
Zoom who?
Zoom did you think it was?
Will you remember me in 2 minutes?
Yes.

The History of the Knock Knock Joke:

Have you ever wondered where knock knock jokes came from? If you thought that knock knock jokes might have ancient origins, I'm sorry to disappoint you. The earliest known knock knock jokes (which were actually called "do you know" jokes) can be traced back to about 1900.

"Do you know" jokes — e.g., Do you know Conrad?… Conrad who?… Conrad-ulations, this was a joke!— were replaced by knock knock jokes in the 1930s, when the format suddenly got hugely popular. Businesses held knock knock joke competitions. Entertainers wove them into everything, including music and dance numbers. Radio stations aired knock knock joke after knock knock joke. There were even knock knock joke clubs all over the country.

By the end of the 1930s, however, critics were passing over them and people decided en masse that knock knock jokes were no longer all that clever. The humble knock knock joke still had a loyal audience, though — one it still has to this day. Kids continue to be the main fans of knock knock jokes and that will probably never change!

GREAT VALUE FOR YOU WITH RIDDLES

What has a face and two hands but no arms or legs?

A clock

What five-letter word becomes shorter when you add two letters to it?

Short

What has a neck but no head?

A bottle

What type of cheese is made backwards?

Edam

Which letter of the alphabet has the most water?

c

What starts with a P, ends with an E and has thousands of letters?

The Post Office

What has to be broken before you can use it?

An egg

What begins with T ends with T and has T in it?

A teapot

Which month has 28 days?

All of them, of course

Three men were in a boat. It capsized, but only two got their hair wet. Why?

One was bald

What is so delicate that saying its name breaks it?

Silence

If an electric train is travelling south, which way is the smoke going?

There is no smoke; it is an electric train!

Why do lions eat raw meat?

Because they never learned to cook

Where do cows go for their holidays?

Moo York

What goes up but never goes down?

Your Age

What is the last thing you take off before bed?

Your feet off the floor

What invention lets you look right through a wall?

A window

What has four legs, but can't walk?

A table

For the last pages of this book

It's your time to develop your writing skills to be ready for preschool and school as well

In next Pages you will find only lined journal to help you being lined when learning writing

Printed in Great Britain
by Amazon